i-SPY

creepy crawlies

SPY IT! SCORE IT!

Introduction

One group of creepy crawlies, the insects, are the most successful animals on Earth. Scientists have managed to identify around 1.5 million types of insects. There is no part of the globe where insects cannot live, and some insects can live in the sea.

Not all creepy crawlies are insects; there are spiders, woodlice, centipedes, and millipedes among others, that people mistake for insects. But all insects have six legs. And then there are slugs, snails, worms and other creatures that slither.

In this book, where identification of a species is very difficult, the scientific name of the wider species family or order has been used. The abbreviation spp. means plural of species.

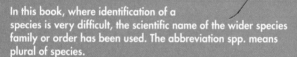

How to use your i-SPY book

Keep your eyes peeled for the i-SPYs in the book.

If you spy it, score it by ticking the circle or star.

Items with a star are difficult to spot so you'll have to search high and low to find them.

25 POINTS

If there is a question and you know the answer, double your points. Answers can be found at the back of the book (no cheating, please!)

Once you score 1000 points, send away for your super i-SPY certificate. Follow the instructions on page 64 to find out how.

Brandling worm

Scientific name
Eisenia foetida

Brandling worms live in compost and other decaying matter. They produce a smelly liquid when disturbed.

What do earthworms feed on?

5 POINTS

Double with answer

Garden snail

Scientific name
Cornu aspersum

You are most likely to find snails on the move after it has rained. They prefer to stay hidden if the weather is hot.

5 POINTS

Worms, slugs and snails

Banded snail

Scientific name
Cepaea nemoralis

There are a number of different species of Banded snail, yellow, brown or pink, with or without bands

15 POINTS

Great grey slug

Scientific name *Limax maximus*

Like snails, slugs tend to come out after rain or in the cool of the evening. They are sometimes known as leopard slugs due to their spots.

15 POINTS

Great black slug

Scientific name *Arion ater*

This slug can be black, brown or orange. Slugs feed on the stems, roots and leaves of plants, making them very unpopular with farmers and gardeners.

10 POINTS

Dragonflies and damselflies

Azure damselfly

Scientific name
Coenagrion puella

The male Azure Damselfly are blue in colour, while the females are usually green.

10 POINTS

Large red damselfly

Scientific name
Pyrrhosoma nymphula

The earliest of the damselflies appear from late spring onwards. This pair is mating in what is called the 'wheel position'.

10 POINTS

Double for the wheel position

Dragonflies and damselflies

Beautiful demoiselle damselfly

Scientific name *Calopteryx virgo*

Demoiselle Damselflies live beside ponds, lakes, canals, rivers and streams, but hunt away from water.

15 POINT

Common darter dragonfly

Scientific name *Sympetrum striolatum*

While damselflies hold their wings over the body at rest, dragonflies hold them out to the side. The Common Darter male is red but the female is more of a yellow colour.

10 POINTS

Broad-bodied chaser dragonfly

Scientific name *Libellula depressa*

This lovely dragonfly has a habit of visiting and even breeding in garden ponds. While the male is blue the female is golden in colour.

15 POINTS

TOP SPOT!

Golden-ringed dragonfly

Scientific name *Cordulegaster boltonii*

This is one of the large darter dragonflies, with a wingspan that can measure up to 10 cm across. They usually live near moving water, where they lay their eggs in the shallows.

25 POINTS

Flies that are not flies

Lacewing

Scientific name
Family Chrysopidae

Lacewings get their name from the network of veins in their wings. Although they look delicate, they have strong jaws and feed on aphids and other tiny insects.

15 POINTS

Alderfly

Scientific name
Family Megaloptera

Alderflies have a network of visible veins on their wings. The females lay large batches of eggs on waterside plants.

25 POINTS

TOP SPOT!

Caddisfly

Scientific name
Philopotamus montanus

Caddisflies look rather like moths but they have hairs on their wings instead of scales.

15 POINTS

Common scorpion fly

Scientific name
Panorpa spp.

These insects are quite harmless despite their name, which is derived from the appearance of the male shown here.

15 POINTS

Flies that are not flies

Green drake mayfly

Scientific name
Ephemera spp.

Most mayflies usually only live long enough to find a mate – up to about four days.

25 POINTS

TOP SPOT!

Small yellow sally stonefly

Scientific name
Chloroperla torrentium

Adult stoneflies are usually found close to running water and although they can fly, they often spend much of their time hiding among plants.

TOP SPOT!

25 POINTS

Silverfish

Scientific name
Lepisma saccharina

Silverfish often live in nooks and crannies in kitchens where they come out at night to feed on food scraps.

15 POINTS

Common earwig

Scientific name
Forficula auricularia

Earwigs get their name from the mistaken idea that they will crawl into people's ears. They do usually hide in small crevices and do not often fly, even though they can!

5 POINTS

11

Bush-cricket and grasshopper

Speckled bush-cricket

Scientific name
Leptophyes punctatissima

Bush-crickets look like Grasshoppers with long feelers but they prefer to walk rather than jump

15 POINTS

Meadow grasshopper

Scientific name
Chorthippus parallelus

Grasshoppers are usually found in grassland. They 'sing' by rubbing their legs against a hard vein on their front wings.

5 POINTS

Tree bugs and plant bugs

TOP SPOT!

Forest bug

Scientific name *Pentatoma rufipes*

Forest Bugs are a type of shieldbug. Shieldbugs have a distinctive shield shape and come in a variety of colours. They are also known as 'stink bugs' because of the very strong and unpleasant smell they produce.

25 POINTS

Dock bug

Scientific name *Coreus marginatus*

This bug is commonly found on docks and sorrels, the seeds of which the young bugs feed on.

15 POINTS

Potato capsid bug

Scientific name *Family Miridae*

The potato capsid is often found in gardens where it likes to sit at the centre of cultivated members of the daisy family.

10 POINTS

13

Tree bugs and plant bugs

Alder spittlebug, a froghopper

Scientific name
Aphrophora alni

The froghopper is a kind of bug so-named because it tends to sit froglike with its head raised.

Spittlebugs

Scientific name *Cercopidae*

These are young froghoppers, also called cuckoo-spit insects, because they stop themselves from drying up and hide by surrounding their bodies with a kind of froth.

Why should the froth be called 'Cuckoo-spit'?

Black-and-red froghopper

Scientific name
Cercopis vulnerata

A strikingly marked species of froghopper, the black and red colours indicating that it is probably distasteful and predators should avoid it.

TOP SPOT!

20 POINTS

Pea aphids

Scientific name
Acyrthosiphon pisum

Aphids are tiny plant bugs, which feed on a wide variety of plants. Score for any species that you come across.

5 POINTS

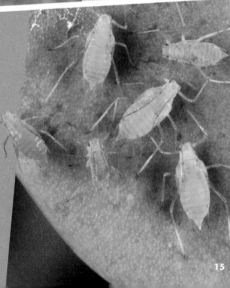

Butterflies and moths

Gatekeeper butterfly

Scientific name
Pyronia tithonus

The gatekeeper butterfly is quite common. It is also known as the Hedge Brown.

5 POINTS

Meadow brown butterfly

Scientific name
Maniola jurtina

This is a common butterfly of rough grassland, appearing in early summer. Its caterpillars feed on the long grasses of meadows and overgrown gardens.

5 POINTS

Ringlet butterfly

Scientific name
Aphantopus hyperantus

The ringlet gets its name from the black and white circles on the undersides of its wings.

15 POINTS

Speckled wood butterfly

Scientific name
Pararge aegeria

The brown and yellow markings on the wings of this butterfly make it hard to see as it flits among trees.

10 POINTS

Small pearl-bordered fritillary butterfly

Scientific name
Boloria selene

These butterflies get their name because of the pattern of spots on an orangey background. Small pearl-bordered fritillarys have been in decline throughout Britain, but you can still spot them in western Scotland, southern England and parts of Wales.

20 POINTS
for any fritillary

Small tortoiseshell butterfly

Scientific name
Aglais urticae

The Small Tortoiseshell appears in early summer and is often seen on the 'Butterfly Bush', the buddleia.

5 POINTS

Marbled white butterfly

Scientific name
Melanargia galathea

Despite its name, the marbled white is in the same family as the brown butterflies and is not related to the cabbage whites.

15 POINTS

Red admiral butterfly

Scientific name *Vanessa atalanta*

This large, brightly coloured butterfly is usually first seen in May or June. Although it is a Mediterranean insect, some manage to survive the harsh British winter.

10 POINTS

Butterflies and moths

Painted lady butterfly

Scientific name
Vanessa cardui

A migrant from the Mediterranean, this brightly coloured butterfly lays its eggs on thistles and nettles.

15 POINTS

Comma butterfly

Scientific name
Polygonia c-album

Pale comma-shaped markings on the underwings give this butterfly its name. Its distinctive tattered-looking wings act as camouflage against predators.

15 POINTS

Peacock butterfly

Scientific name
Aglais io

This large, brightly coloured insect may be seen during April and May and then again in September and October.

How does it get its name?

10 POINTS

Double with answer

Large skipper butterfly

Scientific name
Ochlodes sylvanus

Skippers look more like moths than butterflies. They get their name because they beat their wings quickly and 'skip' from place to place.

15 POINTS

21

Butterflies and moths

Common blue butterfly

Scientific name
Polyommatus icarus

Common Blue butterflies are found on open grassland, commons, heaths and downs across most o mainland Britain

15 POINTS

Orange-tip butterfly

Scientific name
Anthocharis cardamines

The orange-tip is a member of the white butterfly family. The male exhibits the distinctive orange-tipped forewings, however the female is almost entirely white.

10 POINTS

Clouded yellow butterfly

Scientific name
Colias croceus

Usually a rare sight even in southern Britain, the clouded yellow is another migrant from continental Europe or north Africa.

25 POINTS

TOP SPOT!

Large white butterfly

Scientific name *Pieris brassicae*

The Large White is the largest of the three common species of white butterflies found in the British Isles. The other two are the small white and the green-veined white.

5 POINTS

for any white species

Butterfly chrysalis

Butterflies lay eggs, from which caterpillars emerge. After a few months, these caterpillars attach themselves to leaves or branches. This is when they gradually shed their outer skins to reveal a hard shell called a chrysalis. Inside the chrysalis the caterpillar transforms into a butterfly in a process known as metamorphosis. Chrysalises vary in size, shape and colour from species to species.

TOP SPOT!

25 POINTS

Peppered moth caterpillar

Scientific name *Biston betularia*

These caterpillars have three pairs of legs at the front of the body and four 'claspers' at the back with no legs in between. They move by 'looping', a crawling motion which involves the caterpillar creating a loop in its body to drag itself forward.

15 POINTS

Six-spot burnet moth

Scientific name
Zygaena filipendulae

Their bright colours warn possible predators that they are not good to eat. The caterpillars take in the poison from the plants on which they feed.

10 POINTS

Butterflies and moths

Privet hawk moth

Scientific nam[e]
Sphinx ligus[tri]

When disturbed th[e]
moth opens its wing[s]
to reveal pin[k]
markings as [a]
warning [to]
predator[s]

TOP SPOT!

20 POINTS

Large elephant hawk moth

Scientific name
Deilephila elpenor

This very beautiful moth is fairly common and can usually be found in gardens from May onwards.

15 POINTS

26

Large elephant hawk moth caterpillar

Scientific name
Deilephila elpenor

This very striking caterpillar, which may be mistaken for a small snake, reaches 90 mm (3½ in) in length.

10 POINTS

TOP SPOT!

Hummingbird hawk moth

Scientific name
Macroglossum stellatarum

The adult moth hovers in front of a flower and uses its long coiled tongue to collect nectar.

25 POINTS

Butterflies and moths

Eyed hawk moth

Scientific name
Smerinthus ocellatus

When at rest, this moth sits with its wings closed but when disturbed it opens its forewings to reveal hindwings with eye-marks on them as a way of surprising a predator.

TOP SPOT!

20 POINTS

Eyed hawk moth caterpillar

Scientific name
Smerinthus ocellatus

Like many hawk moth caterpillars, it has a horn on its tail.

15 POINTS

Buff-tip moth

Scientific name
Phalera bucephala

When they are at rest, Buff-tip moths look a bit like a broken stick.

TOP SPOT!

25 POINTS

Buff-tip moth caterpillar

Scientific name
Phalera bucephala

These hairy caterpillars stay together in a group when small, splitting up as they get bigger.

10 POINTS

Butterflies and moths

TOP SPOT!

Garden tiger moth

Scientific name
Arctia caja

Tiger moths taste unpleasant and the bright colours of the moth's hindwings warn birds to leave them alone. The pattern of the forewings probably helps to break up the insect's outline.

25 POINTS

Garden tiger moth caterpillar

Scientific name *Arctia caja*

You are actually much more likely to come across a 'woolly bear', (the nickname for a tiger moth caterpillar), than find the adult moth.

 10 POINTS

Cinnabar moth

Scientific name
Tyria jacobaea

The brightly coloured cinnabar moth is warning birds that it is poisonous and they should not try to eat it.

 15 POINTS

Cinnabar moth caterpillar

Scientific name *Tyria jacobaea*

There is no mistaking the black-and-yellow striped caterpillars of the cinnabar moth. One of their favourite foods is ragwort.

 5 POINTS

Butterflies and moths

Burnished brass moth

Scientific name
Diachrysia chrysitis

With its shiny, metallic patches on its wings, this moth is unlike others in its very large family, which have rather dull colourings.

 25 POINTS

TOP SPOT!

Angle shades moth

Scientific name
Phlogophora meticulosa

The dull colours and patterning on the forewings of this moth make it very hard for an enemy to see amongst dead leaves.

TOP SPOT!

20 POINTS

Marsh brown-edged tipula crane fly

Scientific name *Tipula spp.*

Crane flies are sometimes called 'daddy-long-legs' and the weak-flying adults usually appear from summer to autumn.

What name is given to the larva of the crane fly?

5 POINTS

Double with answer

House gnat

Scientific name
Family Culicidae

Small mosquitoes are often called gnats. The males have hairy feelers, which they use to 'hear' the wingbeats of the females.

15 POINTS

Flies

Notch-horned cle

Scientific nam
Haematopota pluvia

Female horse flie
or clegs, drir
blood by bitir
animals, and eve
humar

15 POINT

Black-rimmed snout hoverfly

Scientific name
Rhingia campestris

Identifiable by its bulbous
'nose' and the black
lines on its abdomen,
this hoverfly feeds
on a wide range of
flowers but is especially
fond of apple blossom.

10 POINTS

Long hoverfly

Scientific name
Sphaerophoria spp.

These wasp-like
insects cannot sting,
but their appearance
fools their enemies
into thinking that they
are dangerous.

Shining-faced drone fly

Scientific name
Eristalis spp.

The drone fly is
quite a good
mimic of the hive
bee. Like the hive
bee it feeds on
pollen.

35

TOP SPOT!

Bumble bee plume-horn, a hoverfly

Scientific name
Volucella bombylans

This hoverfly has forms mimicking both white-tailed and red-tailed bumble bees. It lays its eggs in bumble bee nests, where the larvae feed on bits and pieces discarded by the bees.

20 POINTS

Bluebottle fly

Scientific name
Calliphora spp.

Male bluebottles feed on nectar but the female often buzzes loudly into the house in search of meat on which to lay its eggs.

5 POINTS

Greenbottle fly

Scientific name
Lucilia caesar

Greenbottles are 'blow flies', for when they lay their eggs on meat, the maggots feed on the meat – it is then said to be 'blown'.

5 POINTS

Flies

Common house fly

Scientific name *Musca domestica*

This fly is always an unwanted visitor to our homes, since it can spread germs. It can be easily confused with the lesser house fly which is smaller and flies in circles around ceiling lights. **5 POINTS**

Common yellow dung fly

Scientific name
Scathophaga stercoraria

The female of this bright yellow furry-looking fly lays its eggs on cattle droppings. When they hatch, the grubs feed on the dung. **10 POINTS**

Common awl robber fly

Scientific name *Family Asilidae*

Robber flies have stiff hairs on their legs, which help them grip on to other insects, so they can suck out the contents of their bodies. **15 POINTS**

TOP SPOT!

Marsh clear-winged snipe fly

Scientific name *Rhagio tringarius*

These 'wasp-like' flies can be found
in dense vegetation such as
hedgerows, woods and meadows.
Snipe fly larvae live on the ground
and eat beetles and worms.

25 POINTS

Flies

Dark-edged bee fly

Scientific name
Bombylius major

This fly hovers in
mid-air as it feeds on
nectar with its long
proboscis.

20 POINTS

TOP SPOT!

Flesh fly

Scientific name
Scathophaga spp.

The common flesh fly
gets its name from the
fact that its larvae
sometimes feed on the
flesh of open wounds.

15 POINTS

St Mark's fly

Scientific name
Bibio marci

These flies are very clumsy in flight and the males have much bigger eyes than the females.

10 POINTS

Noonday fly

Scientific name
Mesembrina meridiana

The adults of this fly can be found on flowers, especially brambles, or on cow dung, where they lay their eggs. Their maggots eat the larvae of other insects feeding on the dung.

15 POINTS

Flies

Dance fly

Scientific name
Empis livida

Dance fly adults feed mainly on other flies, which they catch in mid-air and spear on their long proboscis.

15 POINTS

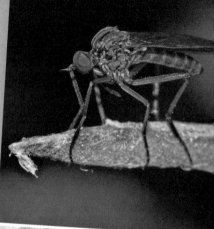

Small fruit fly

Scientific name
Family Drosophilidae

These little flies are especially attracted to rotting fruit and vegetables and can turn up in huge numbers on compost heaps.

10 POINTS

Black ant

Scientific name *Lasius spp.*

The queen and male black ants all have wings and can fly; the female workers do not.

5 POINTS

Double score for males and females leaving the nest

Yellow meadow ants

Scientific name *Lasius flavus*

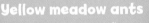

Meadow ants keep root aphids in their nest, which are kept in 'herds' like cows so that the ants can feed on the honeydew the aphids produce.

10 POINTS

Ant's nest

Some ants are nomadic and do not build permanent homes, but many build complex nests. Some are underground, others are on top of the ground or even in trees.

25 POINTS

Wood ant

Scientific name
Formica rufa

The wood ant is our biggest ant. Its nest is a huge mound of leaves, sticks and other plant materials.

✓ **15** POINTS

German wasp

Scientific name
Vespula germanica

German wasps differ from common wasps by having three dots on their face as well as more clearly defined dots on their abdomens.

5 POINTS

Ruby-tailed wasp

Scientific name *Family chrysididae*

These little insects will be found on walls and fences searching for the nest holes of solitary wasps or other species in which to lay their eggs.

 15 POINTS

45

Bees, wasps and ants

Hornet

Scientific name
Vespa crabro vexato

Although these brown and orange wasps are bigger than the more common black and yellow wasps, they are not usually aggressive and will rarely sting people

20 POINTS

Buff-tailed bumble bee

Scientific name
Bombus terrestris

Bumble bees pass from flower to flower pollinating plants. Only the queen has the distinctive buff coloured abdomen tip; on the workers they are white.

10 POINTS

Honeybee

Scientific name
Apis mellifera

There may be thousands of worker bees (females that cannot breed) in one hive. The workers defend the nest and collect nectar.

What are male bees called?

5 POINTS
Double with answer

Large garden leafcutter bee

Scientific name *Megachile spp.*

Round or oval lumps cut out of the leaves of roses and other garden plants are usually the work of leafcutter bees. The bits of leaf are used to make chambers, which they fill with pollen to feed their developing larvae.

15 POINTS

47

Bees, wasps and ants

Sanguine mining bee

Scientific name
Andrena haemorrho

Look out for tiny volcanoe
shapes on lawns and at th
side of earth paths, for thes
are the nest entrances o
mining bees

15 POINTS

Wool carder bee

Scientific name
Anthidium manicatum

The arrival of the wool carder
bee tends to coincide with the
flowering of the
woundworts in
our gardens and
hedgerows.

15 POINTS

Red mason bee

Scientific name *Osmia bicorni*

Named because it often build
its mud nest in cracks in ol
masonry, you are more likel
to see the female as th
male dies soon after matin

10 POINTS

Devil's coach horse beetle

Scientific name
Ocypus olens

You are more likely to see this aggressive beetle at night, but be careful as they can inflict a painful bite!

15 POINTS

Cockchafer

Scientific name
Melolontha melolontha

A large beetle you can spot by the distinctive 'leaves' at the end of their antennae.

What other common name is given to them?

15 POINTS

Double with answer

Beetles

Soldier beetle

Scientific name
Rhagonycha fulva

These colourful beetles are easy to spot across the whole of the UK. Their nickname 'bloodsucker', even though they are harmless to humans.

10 POINTS

Bumble-dor beetle

Scientific name
Family Geotrupidae

The word 'dor' comes from an Old English word which means 'buzzing insect' and, when they are in flight, bumble-dor beetles do make a buzzing noise.

15 POINTS

Seven-spot ladybird

Scientific name
Coccinella septempunctata

There are both red and yellow species with different numbers of spots. The bright colours warn enemies that they are unpleasant to eat.

 5 POINTS

Red-headed cardinal beetle

Scientific name
Pyrochroa serraticornis

There are three species of cardinal beetle in Britain. This one has a red head whereas the other two types have black heads.

 15 POINTS

Beetles

Spotted longhorn beetle

Scientific name *Rutpela maculata*

This very common beetle is a ready flier and is found around flowering brambles, where it feeds from the flowers.

Why is it called a longhorn beetle?

 15 POINTS

Double with answer

Click beetle

Scientific name *Family Elateridae*

Called a click beetle because of the clicking sound it makes when escaping from predators.

 15 POINTS

Wasp beetle

Scientific name *Clytus arietis*

The wasp beetle is well-named because it does indeed resemble a wasp at first glance.

 10 POINTS

Burying beetle

Scientific name *Nicrophorus spp.*

Also called a sexton beetle, this insect is associated with the corpses of dead animals upon which it lays its eggs and on which its larvae feed.

20 POINTS

Beetles

Green tortoise beetle

Scientific name
Cassida viridis

Look for this beetle on white dead-nettle and mint plants. They are well camouflaged and not easy to find.

 15 POINTS

for any tortoise beetle

Thick-legged flower beetle

Scientific name
Oedemera nobilis

This beetle can be very common in early summer and is best looked for on yellow flowers such as dandelions.

 10 POINTS

Violet ground beetle

Scientific name *Carabus spp.*

The violet ground beetle gets its name because it has a purple appearance when seen from certain angles.

10 POINTS

Black oil beetle

Scientific name *Meloe spp.*

Also called blister beetles, it 's best not to handle them as they release an unpleasant liquid used to warn off anything which tries to eat them.

15 POINTS

Acorn weevil

Scientific name *Curculio venosus*

Weevils have their biting jaws on the end of a snout, which can vary in length depending on the species. The acorn weevil is one of the long snouted types.

10 POINTS

for any long-snouted weevil

55

Crustaceans

Woodlice

Scientific name *Oniscus asellus*

Woodlice are not insects; they are related to crabs and lobsters. During the day they hide in cool, dark places and come out at night to feed.

How many pairs of legs does a woodlouse have?

5 POINTS

Double with answer

Sea slater

Scientific name
Ligia oceanica

You will have to be beside the sea to find this relative of the woodlouse. It lives on rocks and cliffs above the high tide line.

15 POINTS

Wire-legged harvestman

Scientific name
Order opiliones

Although they resemble spiders and are related to them, harvestmen are not 'true spiders'. They only have two eyes where most spiders have more.

10 POINTS

Giant house spider

Scientific name
Erategina/Tegenaria spp.

Despite its name, the giant house spider can be found in the garden as often as in the house. Females are larger than males and may reach almost 2 cm (¾ in) in body length.

5 POINTS

Spiders and harvestmen

Cellar spider

Scientific name
Pholcus phalangioides

This spider builds its
untidy web in the
corner of houses,
sheds and garages
where the temperature
is not likely to drop
below 10°C (50°F).

10 POINTS

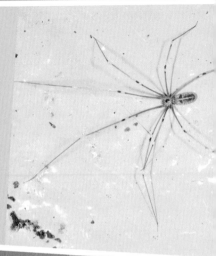

Garden spider

Scientific name
Araneus diadematus

This spider may vary in
colour from pale brown
to reddish-ginger. It has
white markings on its
back, which form a
cross shape.

15 POINTS

Common flower spider
Scientific name *Misumena vatia*

This spider has the ability to change colour to yellow and back to white, the change taking a few hours to complete.

TOP SPOT!

20 POINTS

Spotted wolf spider
Scientific name
Pardosa spp.

These spiders get their name because it was once thought that they hunted in packs.

5 POINTS

Spider's web

Many spiders spin webs to catch prey. Search for webs on dewy mornings when they can look quite spectacular.

10 POINTS

Centipede and millipede

Stone centipede

Scientific name
Lithobius spp.

Despite their name, which means '100 legs' they can have as few as 34 legs or over 300!

10 POINTS

Striped millipede

Scientific name
Ommatoiulus sabulosus

Millipedes have two sets of legs on each body segment, unlike centipedes that only have one. This millipede has two long stripes down its length.

15 POINTS

Toothed pondskater bug

Scientific name
Gerris odontogaster

Pondskaters' middle pair of legs are much longer than the others and are used to 'row' the insect across the surface of the water.

15
POINTS

Water measurer

Scientific name
Hydrometra stagnorum

This insect gets its name from the way it carefully walks along the surface of the water at the edge of a pond.

25
POINTS

TOP
SPOT!

61

Whirligig beetle

Scientific name
Gyrinus substriatus

When searching for
small prey in ponds,
groups of whirligig
beetles scoot around on
the surface in almost
endless movement.

 15 POINTS

Amber snai

Scientific nam
Succinea putr

This snail has
glass-like shell an
can be found all ove
the UK but is mor
common in the south

 10 POINTS

Index

Answers: P3 Earthworms feed on rotting vegetable matter. **P14** They first appear around the time that the cuckoo returns to Britain. **P21** The eyespots on the wings are similar to those on the tail feathers of the bird of the same name. **P33** The larva is called a leatherjacket. **P47** Male bees are called drones. **P49** They have very long antennae, its 'feelers'. **P52** Because it has very long antennae, its 'feelers'. **P56** They have five pairs of legs.

i-SPY

How to get your i-SPY certificate and badge

Let us know when you've become a super-spotter with 1000 points and we'll send you a special certificate and badge!

Here's what to do:

- ✓ Ask a grown-up to check your score.

- ✓ Apply for your certificate at www.collins.co.uk/i-SPY (if you are under the age of 13 we'll need a parent or guardian to do this).

- ✓ We'll email your certificate and post you a brilliant badge!